Along the Avon

from Stratford to Tewkesbury

IN OLD PHOTOGRAPHS

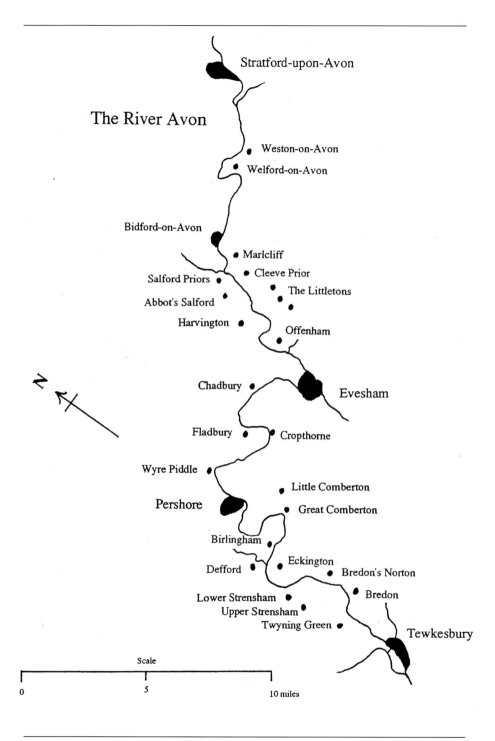

The River Avon

Stratford-upon-Avon

Weston-on-Avon
Welford-on-Avon

Bidford-on-Avon
Marlcliff
Cleeve Prior
Salford Priors
The Littletons
Abbot's Salford
Harvington
Offenham

Chadbury
Evesham

Fladbury
Cropthorne

Wyre Piddle
Little Comberton
Pershore
Great Comberton
Birlingham
Eckington
Defford
Bredon's Norton
Lower Strensham
Bredon
Upper Strensham
Twyning Green
Tewkesbury

Scale

0   5   10 miles

N

Along the Avon

from Stratford to Tewkesbury

IN OLD PHOTOGRAPHS

JOSEPHINE JEREMIAH

Alan Sutton Publishing Limited
Phoenix Mill · Far Thrupp · Stroud
Gloucestershire

First Published 1994

British Library Cataloguing in Publication Data.
A catalogue record for this book is available from
the British Library.

ISBN 0-7509-0814-9

Typeset in 9/10 Sabon.
Typesetting and origination by
Alan Sutton Publishing Limited.
Printed in Great Britain by
Redwood Books, Trowbridge.

Cropthorne Mill.

Contents

Introduction   7

1. Stratford-upon-Avon to Binton Bridges   9

2. Welford-on-Avon to Barton   19

3. Bidford-on-Avon to Cleeve Mill   31

4. Salford Priors to Offenham   45

5. Evesham to Craycombe   61

6. Fladbury to Wyre Piddle   73

7. Pershore to the Combertons   89

8. Nafford Mill to Bredon's Norton   101

9. Bredon to Tewkesbury   115

Acknowledgements   128

Pedestrians coming along the field paths to and from the village of Offenham would frequently use the ferry at the Bridge Inn.

Introduction

'Shakespeare's Avon' flows from its source at Naseby in Northamptonshire past Warwick, Stratford, Evesham and Pershore, to its confluence with the Severn at Tewkesbury. As far back as the reign of Henry VI (1422–61), the Earl of Warwick was said to have been 'mynded to have made a passage for boats from Tewkesbury to Warwick for transportyng of merchantdise for the advantage of Warwick'. Yet nothing was done about making the Avon navigable until William Sandys started the task of constructing locks and sluices in 1636. Altogether thirteen sluices were made between Tewkesbury and Stratford at sites where there were mills. Although Sandys encountered some opposition to his scheme, by 1639, at a cost of between £20,000 and £40,000, the river became navigable for 43½ miles.

The early barges were about 35 ft long and carried large square sails. Instead of being towed by horses, they were bow-hauled by gangs of strong men. In those days navigation along the Avon would have been at a fairly slow pace, as pulling heavily laden boats around the Avon's many curves must have been very hard work. Besides having to negotiate pound locks, there were also flash-locks and the two watergates at Cropthorne and Pershore, plus the inconvenience of getting through the ancient bridges which didn't have a towpath under them.

However, it seems that generally business on the river had expanded during the eighteenth century. An Act of Parliament in 1751 fixed tolls and proclaimed that the river was open to all who paid them. By this date there were about four hundred craft using the navigation and these carried an average of 30 tons each. Besides coal, which was sold along the riverside wharves, grain and flour were among the principal loads, as there were numerous mills on the banks of the Avon.

Trade fell when the Stratford Canal was opened in 1816 and the coming of the railways in the mid-nineteenth century made it decrease still further. In the middle years of the century there were about twenty barges plying for trade on the Avon. Grain for milling was still one of the main cargoes carried upstream while other consignments were building materials to Pershore and Evesham and coal to Pershore. Although a little coal was sent to Evesham by water most of Evesham's coal trade had been lost to the railway. Flour was among the downstream loads, though less than half the barges returned to the Severn with freight.

Under railway control from 1859, the navigation on the Upper Avon from Stratford to Evesham declined into a ruinous condition in the latter part of the nineteenth century, the locks being in a deplorable state. In 1873 the steam barge *Bee*, carrying corn from Gloucester to Lucy's Mill at Stratford, was the only craft trading on the upper river. By 1875, when the Great Western Railway refused to collect or receive tolls, or maintain the navigation, commercial traffic on the Upper Avon ceased. From then on, only small craft which could be carried around the derelict locks and collapsing weirs could be used on the Upper Avon, though the Lower Avon between Evesham and Tewkesbury, under different management and in better condition, continued to be used by barges and pleasure steamers.

This was the state of the navigation when Sir Arthur Quiller-Couch, alias 'Q', wrote about a canoe trip downriver to Tewkesbury in *The Warwickshire Avon* (1891). Another expedition downriver was made by the artist Charles Showell. He travelled more comfortably along the length of the river, at times in a horse-drawn caravan, and later in a houseboat, recording his progress in *Shakespeare's Avon from Source to Severn* (1901). A third Avon voyager was John Henry Garrett, whose account of a passage upstream in a rowing boat can be found in *The Idyllic Avon* (1906).

Passing Stratford-upon-Avon, the two gentlemen boating downstream each commented on the fact that Lucy's Lock by Holy Trinity Church was derelict, being choked with grass and weeds. Further downstream they found other locks such as Welford broken and abandoned. Harvington Lock was, according to Charles Showell, 'utterly ruined, buried in reeds and in rushes'. He observed that Evesham Lock was the first that was negotiable even though it was in a terrible state of repair. Here the mill owners asked a five-shilling toll to use the lock but the artist felt that the payment was in his opinion 'at least, entirely optional'. At this lock John Henry Garrett used the rollers provided for pulling small boats up over the dam and the operation was soon accomplished. Such apparatus wasn't available at every place on the Upper Avon where there was an obstruction to navigation. 'Q' and his companion, artist Alfred Parsons, had to shoot broken-down weirs, though the canoe could be pulled over sound ones.

The Lower Avon was in a healthier state than the upper river at the turn of the century. It was at Chadbury Lock, some 20 miles below Stratford, that 'Q' met with the first lock that was kept in repair. Even though by then there were not very many boats on the river to make use of the locks, John Henry Garrett pointed out that at Nafford Lock, 'Not infrequently a little steam boat passes through the lock gates or even a string of barges'. These craft would have included Bathurst's pleasure steamers from Tewkesbury and the steam barges *Bee* and *Wasp* which carried most of the trade at this time.

Much has changed along the Avon since these three voyages were made and since the photographs in this book were taken. Nowadays there are no barges carrying cargoes but there are plenty of pleasure craft of all kinds, and marinas and boatyards up and down the river which cater for both hired and private craft. The watergates are no more. Pershore Watergate was demolished in 1956 and Cropthorne Watergate was removed in 1961. Many of the locks have been completely rebuilt and Wyre is the only diamond-shaped one remaining. The Lower Avon Navigation Trust, formed in 1950, completed restoration of the lower river by 1965, while the Upper Avon was restored between 1969 and 1974. However, for much of its length the winding Avon, with its riverside villages, remains as peaceful a retreat as these old photographs show it to be. Long may it stay so.

Josephine Jeremiah

SECTION ONE

Stratford-upon-Avon to Binton Bridges

In the early years of this century, although there was a great deal of pleasure boating on the river at Stratford, not many boaters tackled a journey downstream. Voyagers were faced with shallows, broken-down weirs and ruined locks. Passage was difficult at the weirs and it was only possible to get a boat down to Binton Bridges by exercising great caution.

CLOPTON BRIDGE.

Millstones quarried in France were among the cargoes once transported up the Avon to Stratford.

The early barges were about 35 ft long. They had masts of around 20 ft in height which bore a large square sail and which could be let down to pass under bridges.

Pleasure boating was a popular pastime at Stratford in the early years of this century. Steamers went down past the church to just above the mill, then made their way back upstream for about a mile and a half before turning.

The Swan's Nest Hotel, over Clopton Bridge and away from the main town, offered quiet seclusion and homely service. It also had numerous boats for hire.

The fifteenth-century Clopton Bridge was built by Sir Hugh Clopton, a former Lord Mayor of London. Downstream is the red-brick Tramway Bridge. Built in 1826, it once used to carry the Stratford and Moreton Horse Tramway.

Stratford Rowing Club boathouse is adjacent to the Tramway Bridge.

Stratford's waterfront and the river are crowded in this view. On the right is the gondola belonging to Miss Marie Corelli, a popular novelist, who lived in the town from 1901 to 1924.

Marie Corelli in her gondola *The Dream*. Both gondola and gondolier were brought over from Venice and the unusual craft became a familiar sight on the river.

The Shakespeare Memorial Theatre was erected in a dominant position on the banks of the Avon in 1879, at a cost of £20,000. It had a tall turreted tower and a broad circular turret complete with finial.

Destruction of the Memorial Theatre Stratford-on-Avon by fire March 6th 19

A fire destroyed the Shakespeare Memorial Theatre on 6 March 1926.

Holy Trinity Church, *c.* 1911. This view remains much the same as in years gone by, except for the distinctive arches in the centre of the picture which no longer exist.

The arches were known locally as Vicar's Arches. They were once used as boathouses. Avonbank, the house behind, was demolished in 1950 and its grounds incorporated into the theatre gardens.

Lucy's Mill at Stratford was named after the family who owned it. After the mill was destroyed by fire, a block of flats was erected on the site in 1974.

Lucy's Locks, the two-rise staircase locks near Holy Trinity Church, also bore the name of the local milling family. At the turn of the century they were in a ruinous condition.

Binton Bridges was at one time the boundary between Warwickshire and Gloucestershire. At the southern end is a public house, the Four Alls.

The Four Alls landing place. The Four Alls represent the monarch who rules over all, the priest who prays for all, the soldier who fights for all and the farmer who pays for all.

At Binton Bridges there are several channels but only one is navigable.

The Avon from Binton Bridges.

SECTION TWO

Welford-on-Avon to Barton

From Binton Bridges to the mill at Welford there was a deep stretch of river which was very popular for boating and fishing. Both Welford Upper Lock and Welford Lower Lock were in ruins, as was the lock at Bidford Grange. Between Grange Lock and Bidford the water was quite shallow, the channels being difficult to follow in some places.

Black Cliff, situated on a sharp bend of the river at Welford-on-Avon, was an attractive spot to boaters.

The Church of St Peter can be seen from the river at Welford-on-Avon.

The river from the mill, Welford-on-Avon, *c.* 1913. In the early years of the century boats could be hired from the Four Alls or from Welford Mill, the deep stretch above the mill being a favourite fishing ground.

Lazily drifting on the river at Abraham Bank, Welford-on-Avon.

Children enjoying an outing on the river at Welford-on-Avon.

A fisherman standing on the weir at Welford-on-Avon. Welford Upper (Old) Lock was on the right-hand side of the river, at the further end of the weir from the mill.

The level of the reach above the weir at Welford could be controlled by adjustable sluices which can be seen to the right of this view.

Welford Mill with its adjoining buildings made a striking picture. This view dates from about 1908.

THE MILL
WELFORD-ON-AVON

Welford Mill, *c.* 1913. The corn mill was working intermittently until around 1957 or 1958.

Boat Lane, Welford-on-Avon, *c.* 1909. The picturesque thatched and timber-framed cottages at Welford attracted many visitors to the village.

By Edwardian times Welford had become a summer resort, the village being so popular that upwards of fifty visitors were accommodated in its cottages during August.

Boat Lane, Welford-on-Avon, *c.* 1909.

The wooden posts of the late fourteenth-century lych-gate at Welford had grown grey from exposure to wind and weather. Now the entrance to the church is through a modern replica of the ancient lych-gate.

The Avon makes a broad loop around the village of Welford. Going downstream the left-hand bank of the river rises steeply and a good view of the Avon can be obtained from the top of Cress Hill.

On the river, Welford-on-Avon. A small boat like this could have been hauled over the stones of the derelict lock just downstream of this scene.

Welford Lower (New) Lock was about half a mile downriver from Welford Weir. The ruins of the lock chamber can be seen on the left bank of the river.

The remains of the lock consisted of large blocks of grey stone, many of which were scattered. The broken-down lock was often the destination of weekend boating parties from Bidford.

Hillborough Manor. Shakespeare is said to have used the words 'Haunted Hillborough' to describe the small hamlet situated on the right bank of the river downstream of Welford.

Grange Mill. By the Edwardian era this mill at Bidford Grange was in ruins, as was the lock. The weir was a bar to navigation but small craft could be dragged into the water above the dam without too much difficulty.

The village of Barton is on the river between Bidford Grange and Bidford, though it stands on the opposite bank.

In the early years of the century Barton consisted of a few ancient farmhouses and some cottages.

SECTION THREE

Bidford-on-Avon to Cleeve Mill

At Bidford holidaymakers had a choice of places where river craft could be obtained. In summer the deep stretch of water below Bidford was busy with rowing boats and steamers making their way to and from Cleeve Mill, which was situated at the bottom of a steep rise. On fine weekends the mill and its surroundings would be swarming with visitors.

The Falcon Inn, Bidford-on-Avon. There is a tradition that William Shakespeare and some of his friends were once beaten in a drinking contest at this inn, where the local men were heavy drinkers. The next morning, when his cronies tried to persuade him to return to Bidford to renew the contest, Shakespeare declined. He is said to have exclaimed that he had had enough, having drunk with Piping Pebworth, Dancing Marston, Haunted Hillborough, Hungry Grafton, Dodging Exhall, Papist Wixford, Beggarly Broom and Drunken Bidford.

The Mason's Arms and High Street, Bidford-on-Avon. Although travellers on the river at the turn of the century would have found the Falcon Inn closed and the premises converted into dwellings, there was a wide choice of hostelries, among them the Mason's Arms in the High Street.

The White Lion Hotel at the town end of Bidford Bridge was a popular venue.

During the summer months, the riverside at Bidford was thronged with visitors from Birmingham and its neighbouring thickly populated districts.

Bidford Bridge was a congregating place for weekend holidaymakers and this spot was especially lively on Saturday nights.

The Avon is liable to rise after heavy rain. This view from the church tower shows extensive flooding around Bidford.

During the flood of 1912 boats were able to sail on Bidford's big meadow.

Bidford Bridge at flood-time.

Sheep were dipped in the stretch of water between Bidford Bridge and the navigation weir downstream. The weir was made up of two sets of paddles and rimers with an island in between them. On removal of the paddles and rimers a movable bridge could be swung round to allow the passage of boats.

Looking downriver from Bidford Bridge, the site of the navigation weir is in the foreground. The weir was removed in 1955.

Below Bidford Bridge, c. 1912. A punt complete with wind-up gramophone, a canoe and a skiff can be seen here. Among the places where holidaymakers could hire craft were the White Lion Hotel and the Pleasure Boat Inn.

Holland's Pleasure Grounds, Bidford-on-Avon. The proprietor of this establishment, W.M. Holland, supplied 'The Finest Steam Launch Service on the River', as well as rowing boats for sale or hire, swing-boats and other amusements.

Downstream from Bidford the river flows at the foot of a wooded escarpment called the Marlcliff.

Behind the Marlcliff, but out of sight of the river, is the village with the same name.

A large chestnut tree marked the approach to Cleeve Mill.

Cleeve Mill in the early years of the century. One of the chief pleasures for weekend holidaymakers at Bidford was to take a river trip downstream to Cleeve Mill, which once nestled at the foot of the wooded cliff.

Rowing boats and punts could be hired at the mill and there was a tea room where refreshments could be obtained. This view dates from about 1912.

Contemporary opinion was that Cleeve Mill was one of the prettiest places on the river and among the finest for boating.

Cleeve Mill was also a favourite place for picnicking and bathing.

A long weir of sloping stones was set diagonally across the river and this was crossed by a footbridge.

Footbridge over the Weir. Cleeve Mill

The footbridge consisted of a low, narrow plank with what appears to be a rope handrail. Small boats had to be tipped over the footbridge as there were no rollers to help them over the weir.

The flood of August 1912 covered the weir at Cleeve.

Fording the river below Cleeve Mill, *c.* 1915. Immediately below the weir the water was quite shallow and there was a ford used mainly for hay wagons in summer. Lord Edward, son of Henry III, crossed this ford on 3 August 1265, the eve of the Battle of Evesham.

The weir at Cleeve Mill. In 1939 the weir was breached and although endeavours were made by local inhabitants, its state deteriorated. This brought an end to boating on the one-time deep stretch above the mill. Cleeve Mill became derelict and was knocked down in the early 1940s. Eventually, during restoration of the river, the weir was demolished and the ford dredged away.

SECTION FOUR

Salford Priors to Offenham

Some holidaymakers would cross the footbridge at Cleeve Mill and take the field path to Salford Priors, skirting the old ruined lock. Others would walk up to the village of Cleeve Prior. Those people wanting to see more of the river could hire boats at the mill and go down to Harvington. Further downstream boaters could stop at The Fish and Anchor Inn and take a walk to the villages of North, Middle and South Littleton. The interesting village of Offenham, with its tall maypole, was also worth visiting.

Salford Priors, where there were some old thatched cottages, was reached by walking across the meadows from the river.

Further along the road towards Abbot's Salford this row of old cottages could be found.

Salford Priors, *c.* 1912. Brick-built terraces dated 1900 contrast with the thatched cottages. The first cottage on the right no longer stands. The cottage behind it was once the post office.

The Bell Inn at Salford Priors where visitors, thirsty after their walk from the river, could obtain refreshment.

Salford Hall, Abbot's Salford, c. 1905. This gabled Elizabethan house was known as the 'Nunnery', having once been inhabited by Benedictine nuns. In the early years of this century Salford Hall was occupied by a farmer who sometimes received boarders wanting a quiet holiday near the river.

The Nunnery Stables, Abbot's Salford.

Back across the river visitors could take a footpath to Cleeve Prior. There was also a steep lane which led from the mill to the village.

At Cleeve Prior an avenue of clipped yew trees known as 'The Twelve Apostles' leads up to the manor house.

The King's Arms, Cleeve Prior, *c.* 1912. Visitors thought that the yard of this sixteenth-century inn was worth exploring for its nooks and crannies and walls pierced with many pigeon holes.

Near the church low-browed cottages surrounded the village green, on which there was a large hollow oak tree.

Harvington Weir and Mill, *c*. 1906. Looking downstream towards Harvington Mill, the water level appears to be unusually low. The top of the left bank is actually the crest of the weir.

Harvington Mill, a small red-brick building, was in a state of decay at the beginning of the century. The shell of the mill still stands but it is in a dangerous condition.

Harvington Weir, *c.* 1910. Above the weir was the mill farm and its accompanying cottages. At the side of the weir there were rollers up an incline with a tipper at the top for getting small boats over the dam. Below the weir there was a half-mile stretch of shallow water before The Fish and Anchor Inn was reached. Small boats experienced difficulty in navigating this stretch as the river had silted up and become overgrown with vegetation and great beds of rushes. In parts there were rapids which lent some excitement to the journey.

Harvington is about a mile away from Harvington Weir. Like many other Worcestershire villages, it has a number of attractive black and white half-timbered cottages.

This sturdy brick-built villa stands at the corner of Church Street and the road which leads down to the river.

The Fish and Anchor Inn, near Offenham, *c*. 1909. Steps built into the riverside wall once served the former Harvington ferry.

The Fish and Anchor ford was raised at the turn of the century by the local authority, thus creating an illegal obstruction to navigation.

The tithe barn, Middle Littleton. Visitors to the river could walk east from The Fish and Anchor Inn to see the huge fourteenth-century stone tithe barn at Middle Littleton.

The gabled centuries-old manor house at Middle Littleton stands nearby.

South Littleton's post office is in the same building today as it was when this group of villagers was photographed, around 1908.

Harvington Lower Lock, *c.* 1912. There was once a lock and weir a few hundred yards below The Fish and Anchor Inn, but by the turn of the century the lock was in a derelict condition with the lock gates gone.

The Bridge Inn, Offenham. A narrow bridge once spanned the river here. The bridge is long gone but until recently there was a ferry at the inn which was well used in times past.

The ferry boat at the Bridge Inn was guided over the river by a chain which was stretched taut above the water. People in small boats had to bend down to pass beneath.

Offenham at the turn of the century consisted of just a couple of streets of timber-framed and stone cottages with by-lanes leading to farms.

Topiary work in the gardens at Offenham, *c.* 1912.

The maypole stands at the head of the main street in Offenham. The tradition of dancing around the maypole continues here on May Day and during Wakes Week in June.

SECTION FIVE

Evesham to Craycombe

At Evesham punts, skiffs and canoes were hired out to visitors, many of whom came to the town by train. Pleasure trips were made on the steamers owned by Bathurst of Tewkesbury and Charles Byrd of Evesham. Short excursions downriver to Chadbury and Fladbury were very much in favour.

A view looking downstream towards Evesham Lock and Mill.

Workman Bridge seen from Spragg's Wharf, Evesham. The former bridge at Evesham was similar to those still existing at Bidford, Pershore and Eckington. It was replaced in 1856 by a bridge which owed its construction to Henry Workman, Mayor of Evesham.

SALOON STEAMER "LILYBYRD."
Registered to carry 120.

OPEN FOR ENGAGEMENTS *Any distance on the Avon.*	.. *DAILY TRIPS.* :: :: *Terms Moderate.* ::

Apply:—CHAS. BYRD, "THE FLEECE," EVESHAM.

The steamers *Lilybyrd* and *Diamond Queen* were owned by Charles Byrd. In the early years of the century river trips were run from the west bank of the Avon but in later years Charles Byrd ran excursions from the Tower View Café and River Gardens further downstream on the opposite bank.

Diamond Queen moored at Evesham.

Sam Grove owned this boating concern downstream from Workman Bridge. The steamer *Gaiety* worked on the Thames originally but was transferred to Evesham in 1929.

Opened in 1864, the riverside Workman Gardens also owed their establishment to Henry Workman. They were created from the dredgings of the Avon below Workman Bridge.

Evesham Regatta, 1909. An annual regatta, organized by Evesham Rowing Club, took place each Whit Monday. Participating crews came from near and far and Evesham came to be known as 'The Henley of the Midlands'.

A crowded scene during a water gala at Evesham.

People thronged the banks of the Workman Gardens for these events on the river.

The fleet of steamers belonging to the boatbuilder Bathurst of Tewkesbury lined up on the river near Evesham Rowing Club.

Abbey Bridge, Evesham. Downriver from the Rowing Club, a ferro-concrete bridge over the Avon was opened on 29 March 1928.

Upstream of Abbey Bridge boats and punts could be hired at the New Bridge Boat House, owned by Frank Malins.

The ferry crossing between Evesham and Hampton is centuries old. It was once used by the monks and servants of Evesham Abbey to gain access to Clark's Hill, the terraced slope above the ferry, where they grew vines.

When this photograph was taken in 1907 the fare on the ferry was a ha'penny return. This rose to one penny in the 1930s. In the 1990s the fare is 20p each way.

Glover's Island is on the left bank of the river downstream of Hampton Ferry. The bridge belonged to the Barnt Green, Evesham and Ashchurch branch of the Midland Railway.

The Battle of Evesham was fought near the river on 4 August 1265 between the armies of Henry III's son, Lord Edward, and Simon de Montfort. The Abbey Manor, on the top of the high ground, was used as a Red Cross hospital during the First World War.

Chadbury Lock, *c.* 1928. This lock, like Pershore and Wyre on the Lower Avon and Evesham and Cleeve on the Upper Avon, was diamond-shaped. In 1953 the old lock was completely rebuilt as a normal lock with straight sides.

Chadbury Mill, *c.* 1904. Here the river tumbles over a sloping weir. Nowadays the mill makes a delightful riverside residence.

Craycombe House, *c.* 1908. Built in the 1790s on high ground overlooking the river, this attractive building once belonged to the owner of the Lower Avon, George Perrot, nephew of the George Perrot who had put the Avon into good repair during the 1760s. A later occupant of the house was the novelist Francis Brett Young.

Fladbury to Wyre Piddle

The river at Fladbury was particularly interesting then, as now, with two mills, a weir, two ferries and a lock. Past Fladbury Lock the water was not very deep. Cropthorne Watergate was a necessity so that boats could pass over the shallows and into the lock. Before negotiating the watergate, boaters could tie up their craft by Jubilee Bridge and walk up the hill to Cropthorne village. Downstream from Cropthorne voyagers on the river would see the cottage gardens of Wyre Piddle and perhaps stop at the riverside Anchor Inn.

The steamer *Lilybyrd* was upstream of Fladbury Lock and making the return journey to Evesham when this photograph was taken.

Crusaders' Camp, Fladbury, 1914. The tents of the Crusaders' Camp were pitched by the river. The Church of St John the Baptist can be seen on the opposite bank.

Participants in the Crusaders' Camp, Fladbury.

Built in Queen Anne style, the riverside Fladbury Rectory was occupied by the rectors of Fladbury until 1948, when it became in turn a boys' school and a private house. It was destroyed by fire on 1 July 1968.

Looking downstream, Fladbury Lock is sited on the left-hand side of the river. It was fully restored in 1962. Adjacent to it is Cropthorne Mill.

FLADBURY.   10.

There are two hand-hauled ferry boats at Fladbury. One is for public use and this goes to the north end of the lock island. It has recently been restored. The other is a private ferry used by the occupants of Cropthorne Mill House.

Looking from the river, the ferry house is on the right-hand side of the ferry lane. Even today the residents of the ferry house have to keep the lane wide enough to take a wagon.

The ferry house at Fladbury is the middle cottage in this view.

Cropthorne Mill photographed from below the weir, *c.* 1921. Both mill and mill house stand on the lock island.

The two mills and weir at Fladbury. A number of buildings have occupied the two mill sites through the ages. Parts of the present Fladbury Mill may date from the sixteenth century while Cropthorne Mill was erected around 1700.

Fladbury Mill, *c.* 1906. Besides grinding corn, Fladbury Mill once generated the electricity which lit the village street and household lamps.

In the early years of the century the outside of Fladbury Mill was cluttered by an assortment of timbers and machinery.

Jubilee Bridge. A ford used to join the villages of Fladbury and Cropthorne but it was unsatisfactory, especially after heavy rain. It was superseded by this bridge, erected to commemorate Queen Victoria's Jubilee of 1887. The bridge spoiled rather than improved the landscape, though it was of great advantage to the neighbourhood in comparison to the ford.

Cropthorne Watergate. This construction had a single gate, a set of sluices and a weir. When going upstream a boat first had to go through the gate which was then shut and the sluices closed; craft could not move until the river had risen sufficiently to allow passage to Fladbury Lock above. If the watergate was shut a small rowing boat could be pulled up the slope made for the purpose, but if the gate was open there was just enough depth for a small boat to pass.

Jubilee Bridge and Cropthorne Watergate were situated close together. In 1933 the bridge was replaced by a concrete structure which retained the same name. The watergate was removed in 1961.

The extensive flooding along the Avon during August 1912 turned the river at Fladbury into a lake.

Cropthorne. This picturesque village, with its black and white cottages and brown thatched roofs, stretches along a ridge overlooking the Avon. The road from Jubilee Bridge leads up to these cottages in Main Street.

Cropthorne, *c.* 1909. The windmill is no longer on the roof of this building which is now a Church of England retreat called Holland House.

The Anchor Inn, Wyre Piddle, *c.* 1910. Downstream from Cropthorne, on the right bank of the river, is this old inn dating from the seventeenth century. In times past there was a ferry here.

A later view of the Anchor Inn and its riverside gardens.

Wyre Piddle, *c.* 1925. The gardens of the cottages along Church Street, on the left of this picture, slope down to the river. Mr J. Derrett's shop, now known as Riverside Cottage, was both the village baker and grocer.

Church Street, Wyre Piddle. Built about 1450, Avonbank Farm, the tall-chimneyed building in the background, is one of the oldest residences in the village.

Wyre waterfalls, *c.* 1929. At the turn of the century this weir was so overgrown with reeds and rushes that very little of it was visible in summer when water became a mere trickle to the lower level. In this view the situation appears to be better.

Wyre Mill, *c.* 1905. Originally a grist mill, Wyre Mill has been converted into a social club for the Lower Avon Navigation Trust.

Pershore to the Combertons

Pershore is among those few towns and villages which are actually on the Avon. In the early years of the century boats could be hired from the Star Inn and other riverside businesses, fishing being a favourite pastime. Boaters passing through Pershore Watergate might have found the experience somewhat alarming as the current downstream was swift when the sluices were raised. Below Pershore the village of Birlingham is on the opposite side to Great Comberton and Little Comberton and although these communities are situated away from the river, they could be reached from their respective wharves.

The Avonia Troupe at Pershore Water Fête. The poster in front of the Avonia Troupe advertised swimming and rowing races, life-saving and diving, plus a water polo match at this bank holiday event.

A portrait of serious-faced lads taken upstream of Pershore Bridge. Judging from the towels around their necks and the equipment they are holding, they seem to have been swimming and fishing in the river.

Pershore Bridge. The six-arched medieval bridge at Pershore has been much repaired over the centuries. During the process of getting bow-hauled barges through Pershore Bridge, deep notches were made on the top of the parapet walls.

A view of Pershore showing the old bridge with the mill in the background.

View from Avonbank, Pershore. A new reinforced concrete bridge was built in 1928 to take the traffic. The old bridge is now used by pedestrians.

The New Bridge, Pershore.

Pershore Watergate. This photograph of the steamer *River Queen*, owned by the boatbuilder Bathurst of Tewkesbury, shows the open watergate in the background. The purpose of the watergate was to raise the water high enough to float boats over the sill of Pershore Lock above.

This was a favourite place for taking photographs of the steamers and their passengers. *Jubilee*, another of Bathurst's steamers, is shown here.

Swallow, a small steam launch, also belonged to Bathurst.

The stern of one of Bathurst's well-laden steamers.

Flood from Rough Hill, Birlingham. Another view of the widespread flooding which occurred along the Avon during August 1912.

Birlingham Court from the Avon. This was one of several gentlemen's houses in the vicinity of Birlingham.

Birlingham House, the residence of General Porter, *c.* 1908. The message on the back of this postcard refers to one long summer holiday when the governess had charge of the house and General Porter's three nieces, her pupils.

On the river at Birlingham. Small boats were often seen on this part of the river in the early years of the century. The helpful miller at nearby Nafford Mill welcomed boating parties and allowed them to pitch their tents by the mill.

The stocks were once outside the Church of St James at Birlingham. The village, situated in a horseshoe loop of the Avon, was formerly served by Birlingham Wharf which was downstream of Nafford Mill on the right bank of the river at a bend named the Swan's Neck.

From the present overnight moorings, on the left bank of the river at the former Comberton Quay, a narrow lane leads up into the village of Great Comberton.

In this village half-timbered dwellings still delight the eye. The tower of St Michael's Church at Great Comberton can be seen from the river.

Little Comberton, *c.* 1916. Timber-framed cottages and red-brick dwellings complement each other in this rural setting, which is about a mile to the north-east of Great Comberton.

Nafford Mill to Bredon's Norton

Nafford Mill, sheltered by Bredon Hill, was a popular camping place and much loved by artists, anglers and boaters. It was located by Nafford Lock in one of the most verdant spots on the Avon. Visitors from the river could reach Eckington either from Nafford Mill or Eckington Bridge. Below this old bridge the villages of Defford and Strensham are also set back from the river, though Upper Strensham Mill and Lower Strensham Mill once dominated the riverside near the latter village. Similarly Bredon's Norton is situated away from the river bank but was once served by North Bredon Quay.

Nafford Mill on the Avon. before the Fire. 865

Nafford Mill, situated below Bredon Hill, was one of the most picturesque mills on the Avon.

Nafford Mill.

Nafford Mill and Lock.

A disastrous fire gutted the four-storeyed mill during the early hours of 17 May 1909. The horse-drawn fire engine from Pershore arrived too late to save the building.

Long before the fire brigade came, the roof and floors of the mill had collapsed.

After the fire all that remained were the four walls and inside them a confusion of charred timber and twisted pieces of machinery.

The blaze left gaping windows in the fire-stained walls of Nafford Mill.

Eventually the ruins of the mill were demolished.

The waterfalls at Nafford. At Nafford there are several footbridges for the use of pedestrians. This one was built over the weir.

The surroundings of Nafford Lock are now rather more overgrown than they appear in this view.

Eckington Bridge. This ancient bridge, like the one at Pershore, has deep notches on top of the parapet walls, made by the tow-ropes of the barges in past times. Sir Arthur Quiller-Couch wrote a poem about Eckington Bridge mentioning these 'eloquent grooves' which were worn 'by labouring bargemen where they shifted ropes'.

Eckington. Visitors to the river could take rooms at the Crown in Church Street where there was a large old-fashioned fireplace with hobs on either side.

Church Street, Eckington.

A little below Eckington Bridge, Defford Railway Bridge crosses the Avon, high above the water. It formerly carried the trains of the Midland Railway.

Defford, *c.* 1907. Set back from the right bank of the Avon, in the early years of the century Defford had a quaint little church but otherwise consisted of scattered cottages and farmhouses, none of which were by the river.

Upper Strensham Mill, Eckington. The mill house still stands alongside Strensham Lock but the mill has long gone.

Strensham Lock. At the turn of the century there was no one in charge of the locks on the Avon and craft had to get through as best they could.

Bathurst's steam launch, *River Queen*, setting off downstream from Strensham Lock.

Upper Strensham Mill was also known as Eckington Mill. It had worked for centuries before being rebuilt in 1851 but by the turn of the century the mill was deserted, even though it was larger and more modern than Lower Strensham Mill, situated a short distance downstream.

On the Avon by Lower Strensham Mill. Punts were used to carry rushes to be used for matting and chair seats and osiers for basket-making.

Lower Strensham Mill, *c.* 1916. In the early 1950s Strensham Mill was bought as a holiday retreat but in 1958 it was completely gutted by fire. Today a modern dwelling, incorporating the remaining brickwork, is on the site.

Strensham Court. At some distance from the river, early in the century Strensham consisted of scattered cottages and one large house known as The Court.

The former almshouses at Strensham have been restored in recent years.

Bredon's Norton, *c.* 1907. North Bredon Quay was about a mile below Strensham Lock. Boaters at the turn of the century would not have found any of the usual indications of a quay there but could pull into the bank and walk up to Bredon's Norton half a mile away. There they would have found a pretty Worcestershire village, typical of those around Bredon Hill.

SECTION NINE

Bredon to Tewkesbury

In the past visitors from the river were able to land at Bredon but today there are no casual moorings for boaters to visit this attractive village. A short distance downstream is Twyning Fleet where there were once two ferry boats. In the early years of the century this was a favourite resort of boating parties who had hired craft at Tewkesbury. From The Fleet Inn visitors would take the lane leading up to Twyning Green before making their return journey downstream to Tewkesbury, where the abbey tower and some tall chimney stacks dominated the skyline.

In this picture, dating from the first decade of the century, children are paddling from Bredon Dock, which was once used by barges unloading coal.

The old wharf at Bredon, where this group of people is standing, is now fenced off from the river.

The Fox and Hounds at Bredon was handy for boaters, being just a few minutes from the river. It was renowned for its home-brewed ale.

For a moderate charge The Royal Oak Inn catered for anglers, cyclists and other visitors to Bredon. E.A. Clarke was the proprietress during the early years of the century.

A riverside feature of Bredon is this very large rectory whose grounds slope down to the Avon.

Bredon Barn was built in the fourteenth century. When this photograph was taken around 1911 the barn could be seen from the river, but now the river bank is wooded and it can only be glimpsed through the trees. After being severely damaged by fire in 1980, the barn was reconstructed.

Twyning Fleet, *c.* 1907. At The Fleet Inn there was once a large vessel for conveying cattle, horses and vehicles across the river. This was winched across the river by means of a chain.

Foot passengers could be taken over the water in a punt.

The Village Inn, Twyning. The road on the right led down to the ferry.

Whit Tuesday outing at Twyning, 1909. This group possibly came by one of Bathurst's steamers for their Whit Tuesday trip to Twyning.

Both ferries at Twyning Fleet can be seen in this view looking towards Bredon.

The Lower Avon curves around Bredon Hill. This view was taken downstream from Twyning. Rowers from Tewkesbury found the 2½ miles up to The Fleet Inn a convenient distance for an afternoon's boat trip.

Bathurst's landing stage, Tewkesbury, *c.* 1908. At Tewkesbury the well-known boatbuilder Bathurst ran cheap day trips by steamer upriver to Pershore and Evesham. The steamers could accommodate parties of up to 450. The creeper-clad house is now long gone, as are the boat-building sheds.

Bathurst's was situated just above King John's Bridge at Tewkesbury.

King John's Bridge over the Avon at Tewkesbury was built around 1200. The Black Bear, believed to be the oldest inn in Gloucestershire, is at the town end of the bridge.

Part of Avon Lock and the lock house can be seen in this riverside scene.

The steam-powered Borough Flour Mills were erected in 1865 by Samuel Healing. Now known as Healing's Mill, the establishment was modernized in 1975.

Grain was often carried to the mill in Severn trows. These sailing vessels with their flat bottoms and 'D'-shaped transom sterns had developed over the centuries.

A steam barge unloading at the Borough Flour Mills. The mill still receives deliveries of grain by water.

The River Avon at Tewkesbury. Much has changed beside the river since the early years of this century. In recent times there has been considerable development in riverside dwellings both above and below King John's Bridge.

Abbey Mill, Tewkesbury, *c.* 1915. This view shows a narrowboat being loaded with flour sacks. In the background are the half-timbered houses of Mill Bank.

The waters of the Mill Avon and the Severn combined to form a lake in the flood of August 1912.

The confluence of the Rivers Avon and Severn at Tewkesbury, c. 1916. The navigable Avon joins the Severn on the right of this view which looks up the Severn towards the Mythe.

Acknowledgements

Most of the postcards in this book are by unknown photographers. Among the named postcard publishers are Antona, Harvey Barton & Son, C.W. Baylis, William J. Bennett, W. Dowty and his sons W.W. Dowty and R. Dowty, Fearnside & Martin, G.C. Gardner, Joseph Glover, the Journal Series, Evesham (formerly W. and H. Smith), Mallet, Royal Standard Photo Co., Percy Sims, W.A. Smith and Walker.

Grateful thanks to Mr and Mrs A.H. Fryer, custodians of the Almonry Museum, Evesham, for the loan of material, and to Ian Jeremiah for his help in selecting the illustrations and composing the captions.

Hardly any trace remains of Cleeve Mill, which once stood in beautiful surroundings near the village of Cleeve Prior.